Five

Mistakes

You Are Probably Making In Your
Franchise Fitness Business

Clinton Wasylishen
fivemistakes.com/fitnessfranchise

ISBN-13: 978-1517513504
ISBN-10: 1517513502

CONTENTS

Foreword

I've been extremely fortunate to have known Clinton for the past 36 years. During that time he has offered me constant advice in all areas of my life including how to drastically improve my business by working less and living more. He's been my personal coach, friend and mentor since before I can remember and his advice, suggestions and guidance have proven to be priceless.

I'm proud to say that with Clinton's help I've been living my dream by working only a few hours a week while living in the tropics when I'm not traveling the world! I made the transition from a horrendous work schedule and running an office to moving overseas in less than one month and all the while growing my business for 12 years! At the same time, my sales and profit increased substantially and the workload seriously decreased.

I got to this point because Clinton opened me up to the possibility of creating whatever it was that I most desired, then showed me how to turn that desire into reality. Step by step, just like this book.

When I first read a copy of Clinton's book I realized that it was laid out in such a way that anyone could read it, in less than an hour, and transform their business just as I had. It's as simple as that and yet he still offers his personal and experienced guidance throughout.

If someone reading this book does only one of the things that Clinton suggests, they'll see remarkable change! Do it all and you could be just like us, living your dream, increasing profits and working less!

Stephen Price
Dream Travel Canada
dtcanada.com

Introduction

CLINTON WASYLISHEN

My name is Clinton Wasylishen – and you might be wondering who I am, so I want to tell you about myself before I get too far into telling you what mistakes you might be making.

I won't be talking much more about me beyond this point in the book – except, of course, the mistakes that I have made over the last decade I have been in business.

I purchased my first fitness franchise in 2007 as a sideline to my day job, which was OK, but not all that challenging.

That sideline grew in one year from zero in revenue, and no customers, to thousands of clients and over $1M/year in revenue! After four years in business, we had served over 10,000 customers and made millions of dollars.

From there, I decided to purchase three gym franchises, which I grew into over $1M/year in gross revenue. From there I decided to simplify my life and business, and sold off my portion of two of the three franchises, and settled on one gym.

At the time of writing this, we are approaching $1M in revenues, the number one revenue producer in Canada, and number 18 in the world out of over three thousand locations.

Did I mention that I run this franchise while living with my family on the Southwest coast of Costa Rica?

Living in Costa Rica may or may not be something that you aspire to do, but I do want to share with you what is possible. The sky is the limit in terms of what you can accomplish if you set your mind to that goal. It took us a little bit longer than I would have preferred to make it all the way to Costa Rica, but I promise it was worth the wait! As I type this message to you, I am staring out at the Pacific Ocean!

I do not want to make this sound simple – it took a lot of time, focus, and energy, but we are here now. I made a LOT of mistakes along the way – and I am going to share what I think are the biggest mistakes I made. I am hopeful that sharing my mistakes can help you avoid them before they cost you too much time, money or energy.

Before we get too deep into things – I want to make a few things very clear.

First – this is a book based on my mistakes and my experience. It is my firm belief that these things will apply to you and your business, probably your entire life if you are willing to accept that.

But..

Much to my chagrin, I am not always right. In fact, as

you may learn in the coming chapters, I may be wrong more than I am right, but I like to think that I learn from my mistakes.

If you are honest with yourself, I think you will find that you screw up more than you get right. At least I hope you do.

I saw a great quote that went something like this:

"If you aren't making mistakes, you aren't doing much."

If you are working on something, you are going to screw up.

If you aren't working on anything, you won't be making any mistakes, but you won't be accomplishing anything.

Where do you want to be? Making mistakes or making nothing?

If you are afraid of making mistakes, you are holding the wrong book and I would LOVE it if you could pass it to someone who isn't afraid to make mistakes. There's probably someone who could use it within 100 feet of you right now – give it away if you aren't going to use it.

One more word on mistakes – there might be mistakes in this book. As you will notice, I am open to being told that I am wrong, or that I have made mistakes.

If you find mistakes, please share them with me – you can reach me by email at clinton@fivemistakes.com

Resources

I will make reference to a number of free resources as a giant THANK YOU for purchasing this book. To get at those resources, simply visit:

www.fivemistakes.com/fitnessfranchise

Mistake One

No Destination

This is the biggest problem that I see with most people – not just business owners – but the most important thing to have is a destination before you begin.

If you can't picture what life will look like, then you can't possibly have a map, nor even begin driving in a direction.

Imagine for just a minute that you want to go somewhere, but you have no idea what that looks like – beaches or mountains, hot or cold, desert or rainforest.

You get in your car and start driving – that is fine.

How will you know when you have arrived?

You will not – and this is where most people go sideways. Without any absolute destination, they can go nowhere. You drive aimlessly, you will drive off the edge of a cliff.

I have done this before in my life – in fact probably the better half of it I was driving along in what I call "the ruts of life." For the uninitiated, when driving in Canada in the winter, typically there will be ruts formed from everyone who came before you. These ruts are so deep that you can literally drive without your hands on the wheel.

The challenge with this sort of the thing is that you are merely following whoever the masses were. You don't know who they are, where they are going, but you are following them.

Probably to work.

Perhaps to their white picket fenced home, surrounded by snow.

So now is the time to wipe the slate clean, and regardless of where you are or what you are doing, take stock of what your dream destination looks like.

This may be harder than it sounds. What I found in my journey is that I had a lot of preconceived notions about what was or was not possible – handed to me by the people that have surrounded me in my life.

Those people weren't ill-intending, they did want to help, but in a lot of ways they are steering you in their direction not your own.

I drove in my own "life ruts" for a long time, and then I developed a vision. Incredibly the vision I had looks a lot like what I dreamt up previously.

Now it's crucial to understand that I am not talking about just setting goals – this is your overarching vision of where you want to be. You can put dates on the vision (I encourage this). Your vision should be as specific as you can make it, else you will probably end up with something similar, but not quite what you had hoped for.

Are you starting to get the picture?

You want a specific target here. Where you want to be, what you want to be doing, and by when.

Before we go on together here, I wanted to give you my real life example – because it will probably help you with the brief exercise that I am going to give you below.

A long time ago, I came up with my own life vision.

That vision involved living in Costa Rica, where I was free to live looking out at the ocean each morning while drinking my coffee. As a side note, I am drinking my coffee right now, typing this, and staring out at the Pacific Ocean.

Later I clarified my vision to include a family, which I now also have.

I envisioned my children playing on the beach, which we do on most days.

A little over a year ago I was not here, but I am here now, and the point is this – from the point that I created that vision to today was a journey.

It wasn't all sunshine and roses, but I kept fixed in my mind this vision. Today I am living the vision that I once had. Andrea found it almost unbelievable my laser focus on my vision through the trials and tribulations, but I remained focused.

Until I got to where I was going.

Once you get to where you are going, you will have to do this exercise again.

Remember: If you do not have a destination, you aren't going anywhere in particular.

So don't stop here – go to the next page, and work through the vision exercise. This part is the most important thing you can do.

Your Specific Vision Exercise

This isn't going to be complicated – but absolutely necessary. What you want to do is this:

1. Take out a piece of paper.

2. Write "My Life Vision" at the top of the page

3. Write "By (put an achievable date here) I want to experience life in the following way:"

Proceed to write out everything you want in life.

Write in point form, or as an essay. Doesn't matter what this looks like, just spill your guts on paper.

There is only one rule here – you can ONLY write what you want. I hate saying what not to do, but do not write out what you do not want.

Why?

I feel as though I picked up this next example from someone at some point in my life, but I don't know who said it. As a result, I cannot give credit for it – but here it is...

When you are driving, you should be looking at where you want to go – between the two lines and straight ahead.

Your focus needs to constantly be where you want to go, not where you don't want to go.

If you drive along the highway staring only at the ditch, you will eventually end up in the ditch (this is where you don't want to go).

If you continually drive staring at your rearview mirror (the past), you will end up running into the backside of a semi truck.

So the summary is:

- List what you want

- Don't list what you don't want
- Don't bother with the past, focus on the future

Go do this exercise now – then please scan a copy (or take a clear picture of the sheet) and email it to me at clinton@fivemistakes.com with a subject line of "Here's my life vision Clinton!"

Do the entire exercise now before you go on.

Do it!

Mistake Two

Underpricing

Pricing is a fun topic. Almost everything that I have ever purchased from anywhere has probably been underpriced.

As a consumer, I am OK with paying less than I should pay.

As a business owner, it horrifies me.

Most business owners make the mistake of undervaluing the product or service that they provide – and this is to the detriment of everyone involved.

When you make less money than you should, you cannot run your business at the level that you should. You cannot afford to pay your staff what you should be paying your staff, and you probably cannot afford to hire the people that should be doing the jobs that you shouldn't be doing.

So to undo this mess, you need to start charging more.

I can hear the cries from here – even though I am not sitting next to you, I know what you are thinking.

The first thing that comes from your mouth is "But Clinton..."

And carries on from there – in most conversations that I have around pricing, business owners will talk about what the competition is doing down the road, or what the industry is doing, or what they have done in past.

So let's get these out of the way.

Past

Whatever you have charged in the past is whatever you have charged in past – let that go, and let it go right now. I have screwed up my pricing more times than I can count, and I have had to march forward from the point of error.

It has always worked out.

The thing is this – you walked into something, you had an idea of what your product or service was worth, and you stuck that price on your product and service.

You were wrong.

You underpriced things, and now it's time to fix it.

Move past the errors that you made in the past – it's not worth sitting around and talking about, or moping over.

Make the decision to fix the pricing problem and move forward.

Competition

Understand that the people down the road are doing what they know how to do – and they are making the same mistake that I am telling you that you are making.

Now there are at least two of you making the same mistake. If I am to guess, there's a ton more than two, but let's just pretend there are two of you.

If you both keep pushing the price down, eventually both of you will be gone, and everybody will have to move to another provider of your goods or services because you will be out of business.

Does this sound like the thing that you want to accomplish?

I am hoping no – because if you are aiming to be out of business, you had better revisit chapter one.

Check your big vision.

Is there any part in there about being bankrupt?

I didn't think so.

Industry

I don't care what the industry is doing, or more

specifically what you believe the industry is doing.

You MUST align your business with your vision AND you need to have a successful business to reach your goals (this is a bit of a guess, but not much of a leap).

To have a successful business, you have to charge what your product or service is worth.

Now – without sitting down and dissecting your business with you directly, it's difficult to say what exactly your product or service is worth, but we will try to work that out here shortly.

Let us take the example of personal training here and dissect that, as it is HOPEFULLY a big part of your business. If it is not a big part of your business, we are going to work together to make it a big part of your business shortly.

Personal training has traditionally been sold by the hour.

I have trained more clients than I can actually count, and I can safely say with absolute certainty, that unless you are working with an injured or sick person, one hour is way too much time.

Thirty minutes is an appropriate training session for a client, provided you are organized as a trainer.

So now that we have established that an hour is too long, and most of the industry has sold one hour sessions in past (and are still doing so today) we have determined that the industry (and most trainers) are doing it wrong.

So here is what we want to do.

We want to create a package that increases the VALUE of the program to the customer while decreasing the cost per visit.

This is easy to do if we chop sessions in half because suddenly you have twice as much time to service the clients as you did before.

The question is what is this worth? Now you start doing the math – I can see you right now. Working out dollars per hour or dollars per session.

STOP IT!

The value of the program is based on the RESULT you are going to get the client.

How much is it worth to that mother who has spent thousands of dollars and hundreds of hours messing around with hopeless diets, only to end up back where she started?

How much would the transformation to her pre-baby body be worth to her?

Can you answer that question?

You probably can NOT answer that question, because you are not her.

But rest assured you can understand the concept that she's not really doing the math that you started doing above. She's not that concerned about dollars per session or per hour, she's interested in the end result.

If you are doing this part right, you are selling the transformation.

You aren't selling sessions, or hours, or workouts. That is outmoded thinking.

You are selling the end result.

So I have used personal training here as an example, but you could drop just about any product or service into the example.

The key message here is that you do not want to become a commodity. If you are a commodity, you are going to be judged on price.

If you are judged on price, you are in a race to the bottom of the barrel.

The bottom of the barrel won't take you to where you want to go, I promise you that.

The people at the bottom of the barrel are struggling to survive, and for good reason – their customers are cheap, wanting the cheapest thing.

Toilet paper is a commodity – and people don't like to spend money on things that they know they are going to throw away

Think about toilet paper for a minute – there are two types of people, and I am curious to know who you are.

Are you the customer that spends a little extra for a softer experience, or are you the customer who spends as little as possible, because they are going to throw the stuff down the toilet anyways?

I don't know what you think of this example – but I can tell you one thing for sure – there is a downside to being cheap because I have also been cheap.

What follows is my world-class toilet paper example...

You can buy the cheaper toilet paper – let's say it costs 33% less than the leading national brand that is softer and thicker than your toilet paper.

As a result of saving 33% on the upfront purchase of said toilet paper, I end up using 50% more – I have to use twice as much to get the same result, but I only saved 33% on the initial purchase price of the thing.

Now I am losing money in an attempt to save money, but I probably don't even realize what I am doing.

This is what I call being cheap to my own detriment – and a lot of people do this, every day.

I know my example is a bit long and is about toilet paper – but if it was not clear to you – this is the message:

You want the customers that are willing to pay 33% more – because they are the people that see the value in what it is that you are doing.

This isn't about brands or advertising, but about the value proposition. If your customer cannot see the value in your product or service to pay for you to thrive in business, you do NOT want that customer.

Does that make sense?

Pricing Experiment

If you aren't sure where to go with this, or what to charge for your product or service, then I have a bit of an experiment that I would like to try with you.

Before we begin – I want to ask you a question...

If I were able to add $100,000 a year to your bottom line in business while working with you for less than two hours, what would that be worth to you?

What about if we were able to add $500,000 to your bottom line PER YEAR and spend less than two hours doing it?

How much would that be worth to you?

Are you willing to play the game?

I want you to pick three numbers:

How much you want to add to your bottom line EVERY YEAR:

How much time you want to spend figuring this out:

How much you are willing to spend to figure out the "how":

Email the answers to those three questions to clinton@fivemistakes.com and we will chat more about this.

The one question you don't need to answer is the "how" you are going to do it – you see how easy I made this?

Just send me those answers now. Yes, I am waiting for your response!

Mistake Three

No Exit Plan

So this goes back a little to our first concept of having a vision – part of the vision should be selling or otherwise leaving your business.

You need to have this, else you will have a permanent job.

If you want a job until death, then skip this chapter.

If you want to build something, profit and leave, then this chapter is for you.

To me, however, not planning to sell or leave your business means that you are not really interested in having a BUSINESS but instead having a JOB. If you are still reading this, and you feel that a JOB is what you want, then consider me shocked and amazed – my gut says you are in the wrong place (perhaps at the right time).

So the idea here is to begin your business ideally with the end in mind. Ideally you have figured out where you want to be in the end, and that doesn't look like working behind the counter of your business.

Am I right?

So we have to get to work here to figure out what we are doing.

You might be wondering why this is important... I am getting there, and to help with that, I am going to tell you a story.

When I started my first successful fitness franchise, I was the only trainer. I was also the marketing guy, phone guy, web guy, payment guy, bookkeeper and so on.

Really it was a recipe for disaster.

Perhaps you are doing everything inside of your business today. If so, that's OK, depending on who you are, and where you want to be – but there is a problem with this sort of "do it all yourself" mentality.

There are only so many minutes in a day.

Now, if you are expecting some sort of time management system to follow, you have me all wrong. I may be the worst person to talk to on Planet Earth about time management (I am a bit unstructured this way – I have a calendar, and it's mostly empty).

Anyways – the point is this – you need to be doing the things that are most valuable to your business. There is a very good chance that if you are doing everything inside of your business right now, you are neglecting the most important things for the sake of the less important things.

Does this make sense?

The key here is this – if you have an end goal in mind and are clear on what your role is, you can hire the people to fill the holes where you should not be.

This probably includes some of the "fun stuff" that you enjoy doing, but probably shouldn't be doing.

Here is one more example for you – I am a tech guy at heart. I like fiddling with technology, and if I could figure out how to make a real living playing around, I would.

So in my business I find myself sometimes squandering time on technology projects that I probably should not have my fingers in.

Now – the question for you is this – what are the things you are doing in your business today that you should not be doing?

I want you to do this next exercise on a plain piece of paper. It is super simple, but start with a blank piece of paper, and put the title on the top as follows:

Things That I Am Doing But Should Not Be Doing

On the left-hand side of the page make a list. Make it long – because I know you are doing a LOT of things that you should not be doing.

Next, to the right of each of those tasks, I want you to write the solution to the problem – who you can hand those items off to.

Now – if you don't know who is going to do this, leave it blank for now because I am going to give you some tools right away to help solve that problem as well.

Done that?

Now let's move onto some solutions for those items you don't have "someone" for.

One of the most useful bits about the Internet, as it is today, is outsourcing – there is an entire world of people out there willing to do the work that you shouldn't be doing. Notice what I did there – I didn't say the work you don't want to be doing, but shouldn't be doing (there is a difference here).

I use a few different sites, and each of them for different things, so I will give you a few simple solutions below.

Fiverr

This is a clearinghouse of so many things, I couldn't even begin to summarize them all. If you need a simple logo made, or proofreading done, transcriptions, caricatures, and so on – this should be your first stop. Things like simple video edits, transitions, photo edits, and so on. Come to Fiverr first.

Take an hour or so and look through the many things that people will do for five bucks (or a bit more).

It's actually quite revolutionary – and you will find things on there that you didn't know you needed until you find them.

Upwork

If you have a technical problem, then this is the place to go. Web developers, graphic designers, virtual assistants, bookkeepers. You name it, you can pretty much find it here.

What you are going to want to do is start by searching out the specific task or tasks that you want completed. You will then create a contract for the work that it is you want to be completed.

Be very clear about what you want so that the contractors can provide you a detailed and accurate quote.

You will be amazed at what you find here – you can expect a fantastic response if you have a job that people are interested in.

Your next task will be to weed through the tens or

hundreds of applicants to find the one that will both do the job and fit your specific budget.

Just know that there's someone for every task and every boss out there. Don't be afraid to be a little picky, or take a risk if it seems worth taking (I have hired people with little or no work history who are exemplary – and I have also had the opposite experience).

Just remember the old adage, wherever this comes from – hire slowly, fire quickly. Eventually you will end up with a team of rockstars pumping out work for you daily, without you asking them for anything.

Now, you might be wondering how this all plays into the "exit plan" part of the conversation – and if you have that question, kudos to you for noticing that I haven't gotten to the point yet.

You want to build your business with the end in mind.

If you have a clear image of where it is that you want to go, you will be better able to design the business to be what you want it to be, rather than waiting for it to happen by accident.

Step one in this process is having all the right people doing the right jobs – and no, you are not the person who needs to be doing everything (quite to the contrary).

Wrap-up

I want you to send me a copy of your worksheet – the jobs you say you shouldn't be doing, and the solution once you have finalized your list.

If you would like, we can also setup a time to work through this exercise together. I can help you find other things that you should not be doing, and/or help to streamline the work that needs doing.

I can even help you hire the people you should be hiring to do the work if you need that help. I am handy like that.

So email me your list, and tell me where you are at clinton@fivemistakes.com

Mistake Four

Celebration

or Lack Thereof

You might be wondering how celebration ends up in here in the list of mistakes. I have to be honest – this is one of the biggest mistakes that I have and continue to make.

You are best to avoid this mistake if possible, but if you are like most entrepreneurs that I know, you are guilty of this mistake.

So here is the thing – we have victories every single day.

The problem is that every day, as an entrepreneur, we also face somewhat of a shitstorm – I am sorry, I have no other word for it.

So here's the scenario – each day we experience victories, and at least one shitstorm. Then we go home at the end of the day, and the thing that consumes us aren't the victories.

We tend to focus on the shitstorm.

The goal here is to focus every night on our victories and then celebrate them. Not necessarily a full on party with a disco ball and beer, but celebration nevertheless, and focus on the positive rather than obsess over the other.

Does that make sense?

There's a small (like teeny tiny small) chance that the

person that is holding this book is the complete opposite of me, but I am guessing not.

The other thing that is super important to appreciate is that there are two types of victories – big ones and little ones.

The big victories probably warrant a big celebration.

That vacation you have been putting off.

The weekend away with your friends – whatever is appropriate for the magnitude of the success. Just make sure that the celebration is in line with the size of the victory.

There are two exercises that we are going to do now to help you out with this problem, as I am assuming you have a problem with celebration.

First off – I want you to take out yet another blank piece of paper.

Then, at the top of the page you are going to write "My Big Wins."

Then you are going to spend as long as it takes to write out everything that you can come up with that you have done right for the last decade or so of your life.

Yes, ten or so years ought to do it.

This might take a while. If you don't fill that page, you are either daft, or you aren't very aware of all the things you have done right.

Go back, spend at least an hour filling out that sheet.

Next up – we are going to do something that will probably make some of you question my sanity – but you won't be the first or the last, so work with me here.

I want you to go get a blank book to write in. You are going to create a diary. In that diary we are going to do two things – a morning exercise and an evening exercise.

I promise you this will blow your mind if you stick with it.

You are going to start (and continue to fill in) your diary daily – once in the morning and once in the evening.

The morning exercise looks like this:

Write the date of the entry, then write out at least five things you are grateful for. This can be anything – including the fresh air you are breathing, the fact that you can walk, the sun shining through your window, but try to come up with new material each day that you write in that journal. You can come up with five things to be grateful for each morning, or else there's something else wrong here.

Next up, write five things that you WILL accomplish that day. These are not small fiddly things like going to the grocery store, but big things that you must get done, and will get done, before the end of the day.

Then at night you will record your wins/successes for the day FIRST. Then you will fill in what you completed, then follow up with what needs doing tomorrow.

Then you will close that book, and not open it again until morning time.

What you will find is that more will get done each day, and you will generally have a more positive outlook each evening!

When you go to sleep at night you SHOULD find that you also sleep better at night!

If you don't like the unstructured nature of a blank page, then you may wish to make a template of some sort. My suggestion would be to create a binder with your own custom designed pages that have specific spots for each of the things you want to document – do whatever works for you.

You may be tempted to do this on your phone, tablet

or computer. Just stick with paper, I promise.

Do this for a week and report your progress back to me at clinton@fivemistakes.com – I want to hear how this works for you. I know it will work, so don't forget to email me!

Mistake Five

Going It Alone

It took me a while to come up with this one – in fact it took me a very long time to figure out that what I was doing was a problem. And that almost every business owner I know makes this same mistake.

We all like to think that we have stuff figured out – when, in fact, we don't, and could probably save years off of our ramp-up to profit, by tweaking small things here or there.

I had a friend of mine named Jay Fiset tell me a story once – it was about how we, as entrepreneurs like to hack our way through the jungle, even if there's a highway running parallel to our path.

We have our machetes out, cutting our "own" path through the forest. Chop chop chop we go, every day, from sunrise to sunset, chopping.

We can hear the traffic on the highway next to us, and we have words for those "lazy bastards" driving down the highway – chanting our mantra about how the path to success isn't simple, and there are no shortcuts.

We know better than those clowns in cars. We have a better plan, even if it is harder work – "nothing good comes to those who don't want to work for it" we say.

This is all utter nonsense.

Someone else walks into our world and in sixty seconds can see the holes in our plan and/or how we could do things better, but we refuse to hear it. Chop chop chop we go through the bush.

Are you chop chop chopping your way through life in the jungle?

My guess is that you are – whether you are admitting to it in this moment or not, there's a good chance you are going this alone.

Stop it! Stop it now!

There are people out there that are willing to help. There are courses you can take, there are shortcuts that are absolutely worth taking.

Stop chopping your way through the bushes.

A few of my best suggestions (in this entire book) follow below:

Join A Mastermind Group

Find a group of similarly minded folks that are doing something like you are doing. They may or may not be in your industry, but that does NOT matter. From the outside looking in they will see opportunities where you see none. This sort of group is invaluable.

Don't know of a mastermind group, or want more

information? Drop me a line at clinton@fivemistakes.com – I will hook you up.

This is the single most valuable thing you can do.

Get An Accountability Partner

This is neither complicated nor costly. If you have never heard of an accountability partner, or have never had one, you are really missing out!

An accountability partner is just someone who holds your feet to the fire, and ideally you do the same for them.

You are not best friends, and this is not the time nor the place to be "nice" to someone. The point is to actually hold your partner to what he or she says that they are going to do.

You set up real goals, real dates, and get stuff done. Super simple.

I highly recommend meeting once a week and get it done. Each person comes with a list and then comes back with that list done and a new list.

All you need is a partner, and about fifteen minutes each week.

Do this and report back to me at clinton@fivemistakes.com

Hire A Coach

A coach is a critical part of anyone's business in my personal opinion. Without a coach, you lack that third party insight and accountability that I already talked about.

A coach is your mastermind and accountability partner on steroids – this is someone you are PAYING not to just stroke your ego or be your friend, but to be sure you GET SHIT DONE.

A good coach will also work with you to find the holes in your plan or program, then help you fix those holes.

Sound indispensable? You'd better believe it.

Need a hook-up with a good coach? I can help there as well – if we aren't a good fit, I have an arsenal of great people, one of whom will probably meet your needs.

You know what to do – drop me a line at clinton@fivemistakes.com

Closing

I have given you my best advice in as short of a book as I could manage. I hope you have found this to be both entertaining and helpful. That said, I never consider something completely done – so if you spot room for improvement, please drop me a line.

My point in writing this book was to HELP you as a small business owner grow your business, with a small handful of the five things that I think I could have figured out sooner – probably making me more money, or saving me more money than I could even fathom.

If I helped you accomplish something more than you have been accomplishing to date, then mission accomplished. I hope you enjoyed the short read!

Additional Training

I am working on putting together an entire training program based on these five mistakes (and perhaps a few more) along with group coaching calls and personal coaching.

I didn't have the specifics of this program in time for publication. If you are interested in this training – drop me a line at Clinton@fivemistakes.com and I will give you everything you need.

Now… I am going to go celebrate finishing this book. If you have finished reading and participating from start to finish, you should go celebrate too!